Billy Bluefish

HAPPY READING!

This book is especially for:

_____

Suzanne Tate,
Author—
brings fun and
facts to us in her
Nature Series.

James Melvin,
Illustrator—
brings joyous life
to Suzanne Tate's
characters.

For more information,
please call or write:
Nags Head Art
P.O. Box 88
Nags Head, NC 27959
(919) 441-7480

Billy Bluefish

A Tale of Big Blues

Suzanne Tate
Illustrated by James Melvin

Nags Head Art
Number 2 of Suzanne Tate's Nature Series

To Eddie
who lived and loved
a life on the water

Library of Congress Catalog Card Number 88-92517
ISBN 0-9616344-4-8
Published by
Nags Head Art, P.O. Box 88, Nags Head, NC 27959
Copyright © 1988 by Suzanne Tate

Billy Bluefish was big and strong.

He lived in a school all of the time —

a school of bluefish swimming in the sea.

Now bluefish eat <u>anything</u> in the water —
fish, crabs and shrimp.

And everything is afraid of Big Blues
(as bluefish are called).
Even gulls and pelicans stay out of their way!

Billy Bluefish knew of one Big Blue
that ate 149 little crabs at one time!
All the other fish called him Big Granddaddy Blue.

Billy Bluefish was a bully.
Like the rest of the Big Blues,
he loved to swim in close to the shore
and chase little fish.
A Bluefish Blitz!

Billy Bluefish liked to watch the little fish
jump out of the water onto the beach.
(They were so scared of the Big Blues.)
Billy thought it was such fun!

One day Big Granddaddy Blue swam close
to Billy Bluefish in the school.

"Be careful of FISHERMAN," he said to Billy.
"You are going to get caught someday by a mouthful of hooks."

Billy Bluefish was not scared.
"I am strong — I am a Big Blue."

"Oh, there's a nice little fish," he said,
as he snapped it up with his sharp teeth.

But he had a mouthful of hooks along with that little fish!
And a FISHERMAN began to pull in his line from the beach.
Billy Bluefish was caught just like Big Granddaddy Blue had said.

"Now I am in big trouble," Billy Bluefish cried.
All of a sudden, he didn't feel like a bully any longer.

But Billy Bluefish was strong and he tugged
and tugged on that line.

The line broke and he was free!
But he still had that mouthful of hooks.

Billy Bluefish swam and swam fast,
but the hooks were <u>still</u> in his mouth.
He sure did not like those hooks, but he was free!

One moonlit night, he was swimming with the other Big Blues. They were swimming fast and catching little fish to eat.

Billy Bluefish saw the yellow corks of a net,
but TOO LATE!
He was caught in that net.

It was a long night.
Billy Bluefish turned and twisted
and tried to get out of the net.

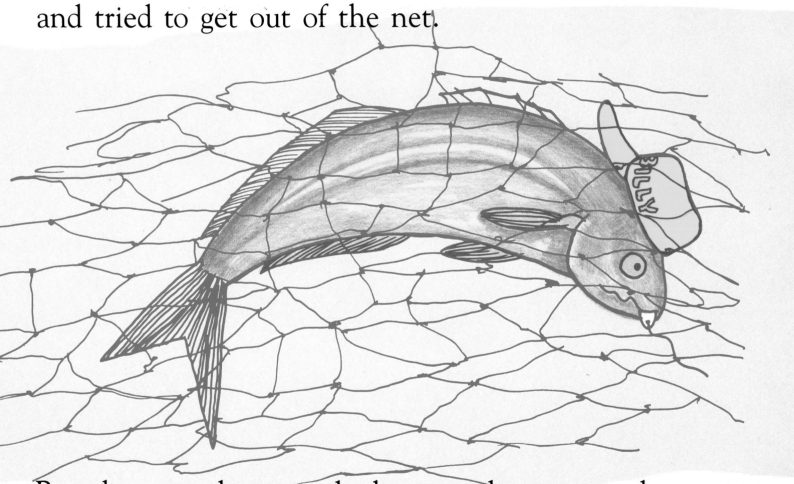

But the more he moved, the more he was caught.
And he <u>still</u> had those awful hooks in his mouth.

When the sun came up, he heard the sound of a motorboat.
A FISHERMAN was coming!

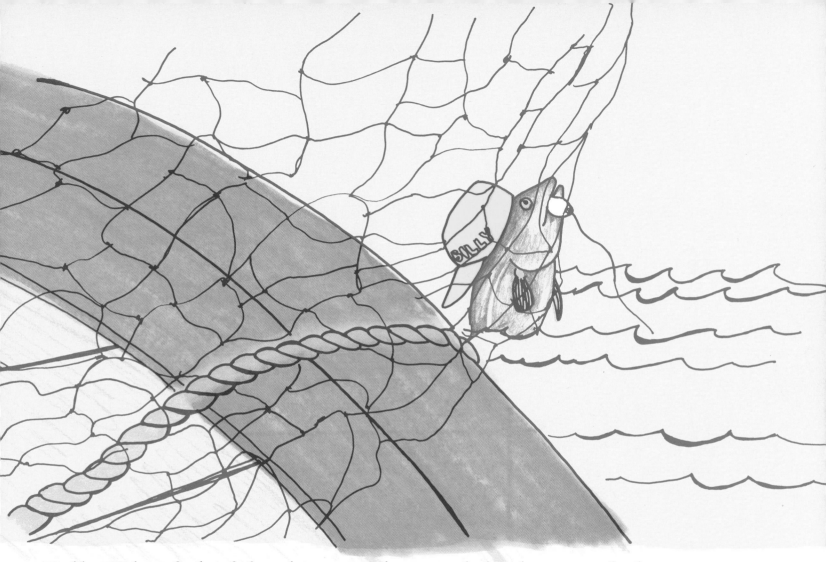

Billy Bluefish felt the net being lifted out of the water.
Oh, how scared he was!
"I'm not ready for Blue Heaven yet," he cried.

The FISHERMAN looked at Billy Bluefish with surprise.
"Oh, this Big Blue has been hooked and got away," he said.
"Well, he won't get away this time."
"But first I'll save this nice set of hooks," FISHERMAN said
as he unhooked them carefully from Billy's mouth.
(He did not want to get bitten by Billy's sharp teeth.)

Now Billy Bluefish could see other Big Blues
lying in the boat — their red gills flap-flapping.
Oh, where was Big Granddaddy Blue when he needed him most?

Then Billy Bluefish heard him:
Big Granddaddy Blue saying —
"Jump, Billy, **jump!**"
So Billy Bluefish jumped and twisted
away from FISHERMAN'S strong hands.

Splash! He was in the water again, swimming fast—
away from that smelly boat, away from FISHERMAN!

Big Granddaddy Blue swam up to Billy Bluefish.
"Are you all right?" he asked in his gruff way.

"Oh yes — I am all right," said Billy Bluefish.
"Thank you, thank you. I am going to be more careful.
I will never be a bully again!"

Big Granddaddy Blue snapped his teeth
and pretended not to hear.
"Come," he said, "It's time to swim north for the summer."